John Poole

Match making:

A petite comedy, in one act / from the French ; by John Poole. The dumb
belle : an original comedietta, in one act / by William Bayle Bernard.

John Poole

Match making:
A petite comedy, in one act / from the French ; by John Poole. The dumb belle : an original comedietta, in one act / by William Bayle Bernard.

ISBN/EAN: 9783337731724

Printed in Europe, USA, Canada, Australia, Japan

Cover: Foto ©ninafisch / pixelio.de

More available books at **www.hansebooks.com**

MATCH MAKING.

A PETITE COMEDY, IN ONE ACT.

FROM THE FRENCH.
BY JOHN POOLE.

First Performed at the Theatre Royal, Haymarket, August 25th, 1821.

𝕯𝖗𝖆𝖒𝖆𝖙𝖎𝖘 𝕻𝖊𝖗𝖘𝖔𝖓𝖆𝖊.

[See page 6.

Mr. Matchem		Mr. Terry.
Colonel Rakely		Mr. Jones.
Captain Belmont		Mr. De Camp.
Shuffle		Mr. Oxberry.
Robert		
Lady Emily Courser		Mrs. Chatterly.

TIME IN REPRESENTATION.—Fifty Minutes.

No. 522. Dicks' Standard Plays.

STAGE DIRECTIONS.

EXITS AND ENTRANCES.—R. means *Right;* L. *Left;* D. F. *Door in Flat;* R. D. *Right Door;* L. D. *Left Door;* S. E. *Second Entrance;* U. E. *Upper Entrance;* M. D. *Middle Door;* L. U. E. *Left Upper Entrance;* R. U. E. *Right Upper Entrance;* L. S. E. *Left Second Entrance;* P. S. *Prompt Side;* O. P. *Opposite Prompt.*

RELATIVE POSITIONS.—R. means *Right;* L. *Left;* C. *Centre;* R. C. *Right of Centre* L. C. *Left Centre.*

R.	RC.	C.	LC.	L.

₊ *The Reader is supposed to be on the Stage, facing the Audience.*

MATCH MAKING.

SCENE.—*An apartment elegantly furnished, doors* R., L., *and* C.

Enter MATCHEM *and* LADY EMILY C., *from* L.

Mat. (R. C.) Eh, eh! ah, you little rogue, ah' ah! I would have teazed you a little longer if I could! but I couldn't, for he will be here this morning.

Emily. (L. C.) He will be here! So! this is I believe about the fiftieth of your mysteries since the death of my poor husband, Sir Harry Courser. Pray, may I inquire who is the happy object it is your will to present, and whom, as usual, it must be mine to dismiss?

Mat. Charles Belmont, Esq., Captain of Dragoons.

Emily. Ha, ha, ha! Spite of these perpetual attacks on my patience and forbearance, and though I am the greatest sufferer from your mania for match making, I cannot help laughing at it.

Mat. Match making! a most vulgar qualification of the celestial pleasure of joining hearts and hands.

Emily. Your celestial pleasure, my dear uncle, has already produced three divorces and eleven separate maintenances.

Mat. Well, well, my dear, I am the author of one happy marriage at least—I forced you to marry Sir Harry Courser, who broke his neck in a fox chase three days after the wedding—so you're no right to complain.

Emily. And having once sacrificed my own will to your commands, you must now allow me to enjoy the liberty I possess, or to dispose of it as my heart and inclinations may incline.

Mat. Ay, ay! That is to say, your heart and inclination point towards a certain mysterious knight, who threw down his gauntlet once for you when you happened to fall into the power of a band of giants and enchanters on coming out of the opera.

Emily. Well, sir, you must own that the circumstances under which I met the mysterious knight (as you are pleased to call him), to say nothing of his person and manners, were calculated to interest a woman in his favour. But pray, tell me, did you ever see this Captain Belmont?

Mat. I stood godfather to him: to be sure I haven't seen him since, but what then? I know his father and family and connections — all respectable—great influence in the north—and happening to discover that he was quartered at Windsor, I have invited him to pass a few days with us here at Twickenham.

Emily. Then we may prepare for a large party

—for we all know what a military visit is; in three days we shall have the whole regiment with us.

Mat. There's no danger of that; in my letter of invitation I particularly desired him to come alone —and above all, to conceal his visit to us from his Colonel.

Emily. Why the Colonel more than another?

Mat. Because Colonel Rakely has the reputation of being a very dangerous fellow among the women.

Emily. Indeed! And how did you learn that?

Mat. From my man, Shuffle, who lived along with him; but here comes Shuffle—he'll tell you all about him.

Enter SHUFFLE, R. *door.*

Shuf. Breakfast is served, sir.

Mat. Very well, Shuffle! Come hither, Shuffle —you know Colonel Rakely—what's his character?

Shuf. Ahem! Is the answer for you, or my lady, sir?

Mat. Eh! what? Me or my lady? what does the rascal mean? answer us both, Shuffle—answer us both.

Shuf. Why, then, sir, he is a wild, thoughtless, dangerous Don Juan. (*Bowing to Lady Emily.*) Capital fine fellow, my lady. Love and war are his idols! and his greatest pleasure is to attack hard hearts and obstinate fortresses, then—as he says— victory is a thing to be proud of. (*To Matchem.*) You did well, sir, to caution your expected visitor against introducing him here—(*To Lady Emily.*)— for I'm persuaded he'd have employed all the arts and stratagems he is master of to render himself agreeable to your ladyship.

Emily. My curiosity is excited to behold this conquering Colonel—invite him, sir.

Mat. Nonsense! If you should like each other what becomes of my project for your marriage with Belmont? No, no! but come, breakfast waits— and Shuffle, do you go again to Flounder the fisherman, and tell him if he'll let his daughter marry the young man I proposed to him, I'll give him twenty pounds as a marriage portion.

[*Exeunt Matchem and Lady Emily* R. *door.*

Shuf. The young people cannot bear each other, but my master is never happy but when he i' promoting what he calls connubial bliss. What a mania! (*Bell rung outside*, L. H.) But hold—I hear a ring at the gate—'tis our intended husband, Belmont! Eh! no! can it be? as I live, 'tis Colonel Rakely himself.

COSTUME.

FASHIONABLE MODERN DRESSES.

STAGE DIRECTIONS.

EXITS AND ENTRANCES.—R. means *Right;* L. *Left;* D. F. *Door in Flat;* R. D. *Right Door;* L. D. *Left Door;* S. E. *Second Entrance;* U. E. *Upper Entrance;* M. D. *Middle Door;* L. U. E. *Left Upper Entrance;* R. U. E. *Right Upper Entrance;* L. S. E. *Left Second Entrance;* P. S. *Prompt Side;* O. P. *Opposite Prompt.*

RELATIVE POSITIONS.—R. means *Right;* L. *Left;* C. *Centre;* R. C. *Right of Centre* L. C. *Left Centre.*

| R. | RC. | C. | LC. | L. |

₊ *The Reader is supposed to be on the Stage, facing the Audience.*

MATCH MAKING.

SCENE.—*An apartment elegantly furnished, doors* R., L., *and* C.

Enter MATCHEM *and* LADY EMILY C., *from* L.

Mat. (R. C.) Eh, eh! ah, you little rogue, ah' ah! I would have teazed you a little longer if I could! but I couldn't, for he will be here this morning.

Emily. (L. C.) He will be here! So! this is I believe about the fiftieth of your mysteries since the death of my poor husband, Sir Harry Courser. Pray, may I inquire who is the happy object it is your will to present, and whom, as usual, it must be mine to dismiss?

Mat. Charles Belmont, Esq., Captain of Dragoons.

Emily. Ha, ha, ha! Spite of these perpetual attacks on my patience and forbearance, and though I am the greatest sufferer from your mania for match making, I cannot help laughing at it.

Mat. Match making! a most vulgar qualification of the celestial pleasure of joining hearts and hands.

Emily. Your celestial pleasure, my dear uncle, has already produced three divorces and eleven separate maintenances.

Mat. Well, well, my dear, I am the author of one happy marriage at least—I forced you to marry Sir Harry Courser, who broke his neck in a fox chase three days after the wedding—so you've no right to complain.

Emily. And having once sacrificed my own will to your commands, you must now allow me to enjoy the liberty I possess, or to dispose of it as my heart and inclinations may incline.

Mat. Ay, ay! That is to say, your heart and inclination point towards a certain mysterious knight, who threw down his gauntlet once for you when you happened to fall into the power of a band of giants and enchanters on coming out of the opera.

Emily. Well, sir, you must own that the circumstances under which I met the mysterious knight (as you are pleased to call him), to say nothing of his person and manners, were calculated to interest a woman in his favour. But pray, tell me, did you ever see this Captain Belmont?

Mat. I stood godfather to him: to be sure I haven't seen him since, but what then? I know his father and family and connections — all respectable—great influence in the north—and happening to discover that he was quartered at Windsor, I have invited him to pass a few days with us here at Twickenham.

Emily. Then we may prepare for a large party

—for we all know what a military visit is; in three days we shall have the whole regiment with us.

Mat. There's no danger of that; in my letter of invitation I particularly desired him to come alone —and above all, to conceal his visit to us from his Colonel.

Emily. Why the Colonel more than another?

Mat. Because Colonel Rakely has the reputation of being a very dangerous fellow among the women.

Emily. Indeed! And how did you learn that?

Mat. From my man, Shuffle, who lived along with him; but here comes Shuffle—he'll tell you all about him.

Enter SHUFFLE, R. *door.*

Shuf. Breakfast is served, sir.

Mat. Very well, Shuffle! Come hither, Shuffle —you know Colonel Rakely—what's his character?

Shuf. Ahem! Is the answer for you, or my lady, sir?

Mat. Eh! what? Me or my lady? what does the rascal mean? answer us both, Shuffle—answer us both.

Shuf. Why, then, sir, he is a wild, thoughtless, dangerous Don Juan. (*Bowing to Lady Emily.*) Capital fine fellow, my lady. Love and war are his idols! and his greatest pleasure is to attack hard hearts and obstinate fortresses, then—as he says— victory is a thing to be proud of. (*To Matchem.*) You did well, sir, to caution your expected visitor against introducing him here—(*To Lady Emily.*)— for I'm persuaded he'd have employed all the arts and stratagems he's master of to render himself agreeable to your ladyship.

Emily. My curiosity is excited to behold this conquering Colonel—invite him, sir.

Mat. Nonsense! If you should like each other what becomes of my project for your marriage with Belmont? No, no! but come, breakfast waits— and Shuffle, do you go again to Flounder the fisherman, and tell him if he'll let his daughter marry the young man I proposed to him, I'll give him twenty pounds as a marriage portion.

[*Exeunt Matchem and Lady Emily* R. *door.*

Shuf. The young people cannot bear each other, but my master is never happy but when he is promoting what he calls connubial bliss. What a mania! (*Bell rung outside,* L. H.) But hold—I hear a ring at the gate—'tis our intended husband, Belmont! Eh! no! can it be? as I live, 'tis Colonel Rakely himself.

Rake. (Without L. H.) You'll tell your master that Captain Belmont is arrived and impatient to pay his respects to him.

Shuf. Oh, oh! my old master, Colonel Rakely, presenting himself as Captain Belmont. There's mischief in the wind; so much the better for me—for, as I know him, he can't carry on the war here without placing me on the staff. *(Retires up* L. H.*)*

Enter COLONEL RAKELY, *preceded by* ROBERT, L.

Rob. I'll inform my master directly.
[*Goes off* R. *door.*

Rake. The tactics of love and war are pretty much alike. I have always found a desperate venture successful. Here, at the risk of being known by half the servants of the house, have I marched fearlessly through their ranks—and, luckily, not an acquaintance among them. The niece never beheld me, and the uncle—

Shuf. (Coming forward, R. C.*)* Will wait on Colonel Rakely immediately.

Rake. (Starts.)—What—Shuffle! So, rascal, you are here?

Shuf. Yes, sir. I have the honour to be Mr. Matchem's trusty and confidential servant. (*Raising his voice.*) May I inquire why Colonel Rakely—

Rake. Hush! sink the Colonel. I have reasons for appearing here as Captain Belmont.

Shuf. At one step from Colonel to Captain! I congratulate you on your promotion, sir. If you jump over heads at this rate, you may hope soon to be ensign. I suppose I dare not expect to be informed of the motives for your disguise—though I have had proofs of my discretion.

Rake. Since you know me—I *must* admit you into my confidence in spite of myself. The cause of my appearance here under an assumed name—my intention for a frolic and a little revenge. Old Matchem has invited Captain Belmont, of my regiment, to pass a few days with him.

Shuf. Because old Matchem has a very handsome niece.

Rake. But under a strict injunction to keep his visit a secret from me.

Shuf. Because you have a very ugly reputation.

Rake. Now this letter (*Shows it.*) containing his invitation and a sketch of my character, not very flattering, happening to fall into the hands of some of my officers, they gave it to me, and instantly I determined on a little revenge. Belmont, who is not personally known to Matchem, was to arrive here to-day. I dispatched him on a trifling regimental service which must detain him two or three days at Winchester; mount my horse and arrive here as the person invited.

Shuf. A project worthy of the renowned Colonel Rakely.

Rake. And now for a little preparatory information. Pray, what sort of a person is your master, eh?

Shuf. The best creature in the world: one who passes his life in projecting marriages. If he had his will there would not remain a bachelor or a maid in the kingdom.

Rake. A true friend to the State.

Shuf. And a considerable benefactor to Doctors' Commons.

Rake. And the niece—

Shuf. Gay, romantic: a widow—rich, and beautiful as an angel.

Rake. There's no harm in that, you know.

Shuf. Now you may be sure of two things: first, that the uncle will propose you as a husband—

Rake. A husband! Well, never mind—and the second—

Shuf. That she'll reject you.

Rake. Reject me—ha, ha, ha! No—no!

Shuf. No offence to your merit—she'll reject you out of pure spirit of contradiction to her uncle. And to be plain with you, sir—having determined to live out of my life an honest man, I can do nothing in this affair to serve you.

Rake. Impudent scoundrel! have I desired your services? On the contrary, I'd rather you would not interfere, and be silent.

Shuf. Be silent! That seems easy enough, certainly: but if my master should ask me any questions about you, and you would have me answer them favourably, I must naturally tell a lie. Now, were you but to tempt me with a bribe from five shillings and upwards, I would not undertake to answer for the strength of my principles.

Rake. Ahem! Rascal! *(Aside.)*

Shuf. You may remember I was once very useful to you in an affair somewhat similar to this. I never shall forget your generous conduct on that occasion. I don't speak of the reward—it was your manner that pleased me. "Here, you rascal!" said you, "here are ten pounds for you."

Rake. I have no recollection of any such thing.

Shuf. The exact truth, sir, I assure you.

Rake. Well, since you've so good a memory (and I suppose I can't well do without you), serve me now as effectually as you did then, and I promise you *twenty* pounds.

Shuf. (Holding out hand.) But I remember, too, that you often forgot your promises.

Rake. Silence! *(Crosses to* R. H.*)* Some one comes this way.

Shuf. 'Tis my master! *(Raising voice.)* Now Colonel Rakely, unless——

Rake. Would you ruin me, you rascal? leave me with him and rely on my generosity.

Shuf. Generosity! You'd pardon my anxiety for ready payment—if you knew how hard it is to gather in outstanding debts on that security.
[*Exit,* L. H.

Enter MATCHEM, R. H.

Mat. My dear sir, I'm delighted to see you—a thousand, thousand pardons for keeping you waiting; but my niece and I——

Rake. No apologies, sir, I entreat——

Mat. Without flattery, this is one of the happiest days of my life. The son of one of my oldest and best friends—once more your hand.

Rake. You are too kind, sir, but Lady Emily, your niece—may I be allowed——

Mat. She will join us presently; but let me look at you—most singular that this should be the little squalling brat to whom I stood godfather—yet I do not retain the slightest recollection of him.

Rake. (Aside.) Fortunate for me.

Mat. To be sure I haven't seen him since he was in long coats, and you have grown amazingly since then, and your worthy father, how is he?

Rake. My father! why, sir, in short——

Mat. I'm glad to hear it—quite glad, and now I look again I perceive a resemblance.

Rake. Curse the scrutiny—yes, they do say I resemble my father.

Mat. Sir Richard Belmont himself! except indeed that he is taller and stouter, and that your eyes are black and his are blue, and then the nose too is different, and again he has a fine round fat face, while yours is long, thin and sensible, except all that—devil take me but its the most extraordinary likeness I ever beheld.

Rake. Admirable physiognomist!

Mat. But come to business, I hate circumlocution, and in three seconds I'll convince you of my regard for you and your family; you imagine that it's for the pleasure of your company I invite you to my house!

Rake. What else should I imagine?

Mat. Ay, I see you don't know me—but no matter, I know you, I esteem your family and—you never saw my niece?

Rake. Never!

Mat. No matter, you shall marry her.

Rake. Marry her! (*Aside.*) 'Gad, I'm not exactly prepared for that.

Mat. The thing popp'd into my head t'other day, 'twill be a capital match, the best I ever made, and the marriage shall take place off hand.

Rake. But consider, sir! Ha, ha, ha!

Mat. I've considered everything, I'm rich and have no children, and when I've set my heart on a marriage I never think of the fortune—you marry my niece, and as I know you can't live upon love, I give you half my fortune; and as it's not the fashion to live in the open air, I give you this house and grounds.

Rake. Indeed, sir, you shall make no such sacrifice in my favour.

Mat. Sacrifice! None at all: I shall preserve my own apartment, and live along with you as a father with his children.

Rake. (*Aside.*) A comical, excellent old fellow this; I almost repent my frolic.

Mat. You'll say I'm a whimsical old fellow, but I shall require one favour of you. The instant I make over my property to you, you will be its master; do with it as you please and never consult me—cut the timber till the last stick, if you choose, but spare the old chestnut tree at the park gate; I planted it when I was no higher than this, and have watched its growth ever since like a child.

Rake. I'll not touch a leaf of it.

Mat. Enough, then all's settled; you have now only to say a few civil things to Lady Emily—at first she'll stammer and hesitate, and perhaps tell you she has vow'd never to marry again; but persevere, and you'll soon overcome those little obstacles—oh! there's nothing like marriage.

Rake. Yet you remain a bachelor.

Mat. The truth is, I've been all my life so busy in marrying others, that I have had no time to get married myself; but I'm a happy man at last, so, once more, your hand, my dear, dear nephew.

Enter LADY EMILY, R. H.

Rake. With all my heart, my dear, dear uncle.

Emily. (*Overhearing.*) Dear uncle! there—I'm already married.

Mat. Ah! Lady Emily! Captain Belmont, my niece.

Rake. I hope Lady Emily will allow me to offer her the assurance of my entire devotion.

Emily. (*With cold politeness.*) You do me honour, sir.

Mat. (*To Lady Emily.*) Well, what do you think of him?

Emily. Really I see nothing extraordinary in him.

Mat. Don't you! 'Gad, you will, though, by and bye, for all that!

Rake. She's charming! (*Aside.*)

Mat. (*To Rakely.*) Well, what do you say? I didn't deceive you? Young, handsome, and a widow—it all now depends upon yourself.

Emily. By that confidential whisper I judge everything is arranged between them.

Mat. Now, my dear Captain, I must leave you. (*With emphasis, looking at Lady Emily.*) But I shall make no apologies for my absence—this is liberty hall, and in the country we use no ceremony. (*Whispers.*) Remember, Belmont, it all depends upon yourself. (*To Lady Emily.*) Recollect this is the son of my oldest friend, you understand. (*She turns away.*) 'Tis done! they are inspired with a mutual passion—I read it in their eyes.

[*Exit* D. *in* F.

Rake. How deeply I am indebted to Mr. Matchem, madam, for allowing me an opportunity of a conversation with you.

Emily. Listen to me, sir! I love my uncle and esteem him, but I am growing weary of his ridiculous mania of attempting to marry me to the first person that happens to fall in his way.

Rake. How?

Emily. I'm not mistaken. I'm persuaded that already the preliminaries are arranged. Come, be candid—has he not induced you to hope that you will easily obtain my heart?

Rake. I confess it.

Emily. And no doubt you believe all he has told you. (*Seriously, and with decision.*) But let me add that if I am destined again to lose my liberty, the miracle is not to be accomplished by his officious interference, I assure you.

Rake. So young, so beautiful, yet so severe! Ah, madam, ere you pronounce——

Emily. (*Gaily.*) Pray spare yourself the trouble of what you were about to say—I know it by anticipation. "I, of all your admirers, lovely Lady Emily, am the most sincere, the most devoted; mine is no fugitive passion; the instant I beheld those eyes my heart experienced an emotion till then unknown—etcetera, etcetera—etcetera, etcetera.

Rake. (*Aside.*) Ha, ha, ha! I could stand a formal refusal—that would leave me hopes, but zounds! to be laughed at will kill me.

Emily. Now, is not this a tolerable report of your intended speech? Thanks to Mr. Matchem, since my widowhood I have been so accustomed to listen to these addresses, and have found them all so much of a family, that I'm certain of the fidelity of my anticipation—at best, they are but tiresome variations on a very dull air—ha, ha, ha!

Rake. (*Aside.*) Curse me, but her gaiety has so completely overthrown me that I know not what to say. Madam, if you reject me, you drive me to despair, and I swear——

Emily. Pray don't, sir; all you can say is useless —I love to be frank, and confess that, inasmuch as I dislike by anticipation all the parties proposed to me by my uncle, I feel predisposed in favour of that colonel—Colonel Rakely, whom he has forbidden his door—though I dare say the poor gentleman never had a thought of presenting himself at it.

Rake. Is it possible? And can Colonel Rakely hope——

Emily. I do not confess so much—and if I feel somewhat favourably disposed towards him it is because he has not the demerit of having been presented to me by my uncle.

Rake. (*Aside.*) Devil take my borrowed captaincy, I should have succeeded in my own character—I'll confess all. Lady Emily, you are deceived, and on my knees I avow to you—

Enter MATCHEM, D. in F.

Emily. Sir, rise! Rise, sir, I beg!

Rake. Will you pardon me, when I declare that I am——

Emily. I entreat, sir, you will quit that position.

Mat. (*Coming forward.*) Well done, young man. (*To Lady Emily.*) Now, then, at length, I hope you will allow that it is possible for me to succeed in making a match.

Emily. Ask Mr. Belmont his opinion on the subject.

Rake. Why, faith, sir, I have no reason to complain.

Mat. That's well—this time I have hit it, however, or I am mightily mistaken.

Enter SHUFFLE, L. H.

Shuf. (*To Matchem.*) An officer of the same regiment as this gentleman desires to see you, sir.

Emily. Another suitor!

Mat. Eh? What! An officer of—one of your friends whom you have invited—oh?

Rake. Not I, sir! 'Tis sufficient that I have presumed to present myself.

Mat. And who is the gentleman?

Shuf. Captain Belmont, sir.

Rake. (*Aside.*) Undermined and exploded, by heaven!

Mat. Belmont—Captain Belmont! Nonsense: he makes a mistake: that can't be his name—ask him again.

Emily. Is there another Captain Belmont in your regiment, sir?

Mat. Ay—is there another Captain Belmont in your regiment, sir?

Emily. You appear embarrassed.

Rake. Why, really, madam, this is so singular an occurrence.

Mat. We'll not admit him until I have examined him a little about this affair.

Rake. Right, sir, right—we'll not admit him.

Shuf. I'll tell him you're engaged, sir.

(*Going.*)

Mat. No—stay you here; I have occasion for you—ring the bell. (*Shuffle rings.*)

Enter ROBERT, L. H.

Robert, tell the gentleman who waits I can't receive him at present. [*Exit Robert, L.H.*] This is a very extraordinary event. I hardly know—by the bye, your colonel, Colonel Rakely—it is likely he has discovered you are here?

Rake. Not at all improbable.

Mat. He's young and enterprising.

Rake. And would undertake anything where a pretty woman is in the question.

Shuf. And should he have discovered the little liberties you allowed yourself with his reputation in your letter to Captain Belmont, perhaps, in revenge, he may have——

Mat. I see it at once. (*To Shuffle.*) But I am indebted to you for all I know about Colonel Rakely.

Shuf. (*Looking slyly at Rakely.*) And that very little to his credit, sir.

Emily. Should it be he—ha! ha, ha!

Mat. But, in consideration, Shuffle, it can't be; for you served him many years, and would have recognised him.

Shuf. (*Affecting embarrassment.*) Recognised him—true; but the length of time since—besides, my memory sometimes fails me and—and then, my honour, sir.

Mat. I see how it is. You're a rogue, and have received a bribe to hold your tongue.

Shuf. I have received nothing, I assure you, sir,—(*Looking significantly at Rakely.*)—except a promise.

Mat. Now, sirrah, tell me the whole truth of this affair, or this instant I'll turn you out of doors.

Shuf. Well, sir, since you insist I will tell you. The moment the Colonel approached I knew him.

(*The Colonel winks, &c., to Shuffle.*)

Mat. Go on, sir.

Shuf. He leaps from his horse, rings at the gate and desires a servant to announce him as Captain Belmont.

Mat. So! so!

Shuf. I present myself—the instant he beholds me, he recollects me—I perceive his confusion. (*Rakely makes signs to Shuffle.*) He nods, winks, and makes signs to me, as hints not to betray him.

Mat. Very pretty! he makes signs too.

Shuf. But I, like a faithful servant, pretend not to observe them, (*Rakely impatient.*) He becomes impatient.

Emily. Then there were persons present?

Shuf. Two, my lady, whose presence is very distressing to him.

Mat. Come, what follows?

Rake. (*Aside, and touches Shuffle's elbow.*) Twenty pounds on the success of my scheme.

Shuf. With the greatest caution he approaches, touches my elbow, and whispers "twenty pounds on the success of my scheme."

Mat. (C.) I see it all before me.

Rake. (L.) So do I.

Emily. (R.) The Colonel is generous, it appears.

Shuf. In promises, my lady—but I have not got them yet—I, who am not to be taken in with fine words, turn a deaf ear to him; he perceives the cause of my backwardness to serve him—puts his hand into his pocket,—(*With emphasis on each word, and looks at Rakely.*)—he puts his hand into his pocket. (*Rakely rubs his hands negligently together.*) No, I'm out! He does not put his hand into his pocket just yet.

Rake. (*Aside.*) The rascal will be too strong for me.

Mat. Quick, and make an end.

Emily. Why all these trifling details?

Shuf. They are absolutely necessary, my lady. (*Pointedly and keeping his eye fixedly upon Rakely.*) I give the disguised to understand his fate depends on me; he feels the value of the hint: it produces the effect intended, and thus with evident reluctance he pulls out his purse.

Mat. Well, well, he gives it to you.

Shuf. Not immediately, sir, on account of the two persons I mentioned—but he takes the opportunity of a moment when they don't observe. (*Lady Emily and Matchem whisper.*) I dexterously put my hand behind me, seize the purse, and here it is.

Mat. (*To Lady Emily.*) I told you what a terrible fellow this Colonel was.

Emily. For my part, I am amused at his enterprize.

Mat. Indeed! Retire, my dear, I must consider what steps I had best take in this affair.

Rake. (*Crossing to Matchem,* R.) Consider he is my colonel—if we meet, as I cannot always command my temper, I may be led to transgress the laws of military subordination; on his account, therefore, as well as mine, I advise you not to receive him.

Mat. Right! I will not receive him.

Emily. Now, I am of a different opinion—receive him, and receive him, too, with an air of cordiality, and if you would be thoroughly revenged for the deception he would pass on you—leave him to me.

Mat. Right! I will receive him.

Rake. Be assured, sir, his presence will be dangerous.

Emily. You appear strangely troubled at the idea of meeting him. Well, do as you please, but I give you fair warning that I'm determined to see him.

Mat. I'll not allow——

Emily. Hark'ye, my dear uncle : if you wish me to take an aversion to him, you know how to succeed.

Mat. How?

Emily. Do you present him to me.

[*Exit* C. and L.

Enter ROBERT, L. H.

Rob. Captain Belmont.

[*Exit* L. H.

Rake. Lady Emily is predisposed in the Colonel's favour ; if you admit him, farewell to your project and mine.

Mat. This is an awkward situation for me ; the forms observed by good society—his family—his rank as colonel ; suppose you go to him and explain.

Shuf. How, sir! would you be the occasion of an unhappy quarrel ? *A meeting* would be fatal ! (*To Rakely.*) Take a turn or two round the grounds, sir, and in that time my master and I——

Mat. Right! do so, and I and Shuffle will arrange the affair during your absence.

Rake. Right! but whatever you do, the result must be his dismissal.

Mat. It shall.

Rake. (*Aside to Shuffle.*) Now endeavour, rascal, to earn the money you have already received.

[*Exit Rakely,* C.

Mat. Now, let me see—let me see! so, my mind is made up ; present my compliments to Colonel Rakely and request him——

Shuf. To mount his horse and vanish. (*Going.*)

Mat. No, no, to walk in. I'll read him a lecture that shall electrify him.

Shuf. (*Aside.*) Zounds, that will never do ! Avoid an explanation ; I know him, he's a terrible fellow ; you yourself, (you'll pardon me), are not very to operate in dispute—you grow angry, he flies in a passion, he calls you out, blows out your brains, picks a quarrel with his rival, shoots him, says a few fine things in excuse to Lady Emily and carries her off.

Mat. Why Shuffle—Shuffle ! this Colonel must be either a devil, or a hero in a melo-drama ; if he's such a terrible dog, what can you do ?

Shuf. Everything. I know him well ; spite of his little faults he's a good-hearted soul ; besides I have an infinite regard for me. I'll talk to him as a father, I'll give him a touch of the pathetic. " Colonel," will I say, " what the devil brings you

here ? why come to disturb the peace of a respectable family ? why would you destroy the happiness of a quiet elderly gentleman, whose only remaining wish is to see his niece well married and then to descend with honour to the grave." (*Matchem draws his hand over his eyes.*) " Colonel, dear and respected Colonel, will you never keep your d—d fingers out of other men's dishes." This speech produces its intended effect, he sheds one tear, presses my hand, mounts his horse and gallops away ; I return and announce his departure : you overjoy'd at the success of my embassy, offer me a few guineas—I refuse—you insist, and I accept ; and thus is the affair brought to a peaceable conclusion.

Mat. Well, be it as you propose. Shuffle, you're an honest fellow, a faithful servant, and as a reward for your attachment to me——

Shuf. Sir, don't imagine it is for interest's sake.

Mat. Not at all, but as a recompense for your attachment to me—I'll look out for a good little wife for you.

Shuf. Hang the reward, sir.

Bel. (*Speaks without,* L. H.) Don't tell me, sirrah, I am determined to see your master.

Shuf. Here he comes, now leave me alone with him, and I'll despatch him in a twinkling.

Mat. But I must have a peep, just to see what sort of a——

Shuf. Now pray retire—Quick, quick !

[*Exit Matchem,* R. H.

All's right again, I'm in a bright way to-day, the Colonel has paid me for assisting him, my master shall pay me for deceiving him, and my Captain yonder shall reward my address in sending him about his business.

Enter CAPTAIN BELMONT, L. H

Bel. Pretty treatment this to a gentleman whom he invites to his house. To keep me cooling my heels half an hour in the hall. (*Perceives Shuffle.*) So, do you belong to the house?

Shuf. At your service, sir.

Bel. Perhaps you can explain to me why Mr. Matchem refuses to receive me ?

Shuf. I imagine, sir, it's because he don't choose it.

Bel. What! he invites me to pass a few days with him, I accept his invitation, and this is his mode of treating my visit. There is some mystery.

Shuf. Mystery! profound!

Bel. Which you can develope to me.

Shuf. Impossible—I am forbidden under a threat of being turned out of my place, to utter a word on the subject—I am but a poor lad, sir, with nothing but my place, and probity for my fortune, and though together they don't amount to much, yet as you are a stranger——

Bel. I understand. I am not rich enough to purchase your probity, but if I were to offer you a recompense for the loss of your place——

Shuf. Why then, sir, the other half of my fortune would be in a very ticklish position.

Bel. (*Taking money from purse.*) Will this unseal your lips?

Shuf. (*Taking money.*) We may begin to chat a little on the subject.

Bel. First, then, the reason of Mr. Matchem's extraordinary conduct after the kind letter I received from him?

Shuf. Why, sir, the fact is, the family have taken

it into their heads that you are not yourself, that you are not Captain Belmont.

Bel. Who the devil am I then?

Shuf. Why, they will have it you are a Colonel Rakely, a dissipated——

Bel. Ridiculous! Who could have raised so absurd a report?

Shuf. Why, sir, as I suspect, a certain servant, who formerly lived with the Colonel. Now Mr. Matchem having taken a dislike to that gentleman——

Bel. Refuses to see me.

Shuf. Exactly so.

Bel. As to the servant—he is a rascal.

Shuf. I can say nothing to the contrary.

Bel. He has been bought.

Shuf. (*Mysteriously.*) By a rival, perhaps.

Bel. A rival!

Shuf. Some adventurer, presuming on the old gentleman's ignorance of your person, has——

Bel. I perceive—presented himself in my name.

Shuf. That is it, sir, and the rascal of a servant we talked of, has favoured the deception.

Bel. And he has the effrontery to maintain that I am Colonel Rakely?

Shuf. Even so; and now, sir, you are acquainted with the whole history, I have only to add that Mr. Matchem, firmly persuaded that you are the Colonel, has sent me to request that you will—

Bel. Go about my business!

Shuf. That is the sum total of his message, and I am sure you feel the necessity of—

Bel. Remaining here, fixed and immovable, spite of his civil request.

Shuf. Remaining !—then I'm ruined. (*Aside.*) But, sir, he is irritated to such a degree——

Bel. No matter—I'll talk to him.

Shuf. He'll require proofs of your identity.

Bel. I have certain papers about me, that——

Shuf. The devil! He'll not consider them; let me advise you to go. sir.

Bel. No; here I stay; I shall find it easy to convince him of his error, the pretender will be compelled to retire, and the knave of a servant will incontinently be kicked out of doors.

Shuf. So! I have a pretty prospect before me. (*Aside.*) Now, sir, if I could but prevail on you—zounds, here's my master! What's to be done?

MATCHEM enters, R. H.

If you are determined to stay, I'll just say a word or two in your favour.

Mat. (*Aside to Shuffle.*) What, not gone yet?

Shuf. My pathos is all thrown away upon him, he persists in passing himself as Belmont.

Mat. And has he the assurance to imagine he can impose on me?

Shuf. He says he is certain of it, you are such a quiet easy sort of a person.

Mat. He takes me then for an absolute noodle?

Shuf. So it seems, sir; well, I leave him to you; get rid of him if you can. The players have both paid card money, (*touching his pockets,*) so win who can.   [*Exit, R. H.*

Bel. Mr. Matchem, it appears there is some little mistake with regard to me.

Mat. Sir, you are too late; I conceive how mortifying it must be to a man of your celebrity to fail of imposing on a quiet easy sort of a person, like myself; but we know you, Colonel, we know you.

Bel. Colonel! Thank you for my promotion, sir —but I assure you, you are deceived. I wait on you in consequence of this letter.

Mat. Ay, my letter—let me see my letter.

Bel. (*Searching his pocket book.*) Why no! that's not it—why, where can it be, but no matter.

Mat. Ha, ha, ha! No matter, as you say.

Bel. Really this is very provoking—I repeat that I am here in consequence of your own invitation, Mr. Matchem, and as the son of your old friend, my father, whom you well know——

Mat. (*Sharply,*) Your father, sir, I don't know him—never knew him.

Bel. How! not know Sir Richard Belmont?

Mat. Oh, yes! I know Sir Richard Belmont, and esteem him; but he is not your father.

Bel. Then pray, sir, who is my father?

Mat. That's a question, I wouldn't undertake to answer to a son of my own, if I had one.

Bel. Sir, I swear——

Mat. By all the birds in the air, if you please—and I'll not believe you.

Bel. But, sir, I can show you proofs.

Mat. Proofs, ha, ha, ha! papers eh! ha, ha, ha!

Bel. Papers, if you please. (*takes out pocket book.*) There, sir, convince yourself.

Mat. I'll not look at one of them, not I.

Bel. This is too much.

Mat. The battle is lost, Colonel, and, as a good soldier, you should endeavour to make an honourable retreat; quit your masquerade, abandon the name of Belmont, and announce yourself in your own, and I shall be proud to receive you as Colonel Rakely.

Bel. Sir, I should blush to assume a name and rank to which I have no claim, and should be unworthy the honour of your friendship were I to accept your invitation on the terms you propose—sir, I take my leave and hope to convince you of your error.   [*Exit, L. H.*

Mat. That young fellow pleases me—'gad, he made a hard fight, and maintaining his ground as he did, shows him to be a lad of spirit; there's something too in his manners and appearance that attached me at first sight, (*reflecting.*)—should he really be in love with my niece—should his intentions really be as it were matrimonial—he is a man of family, a Colonel of Dragoons—eh! why now it would be precisely—I'll not be in haste to conclude with Belmont—this would be a much better match.

Enter LADY EMILY, L. H.

Emily. Dear sir, you will hardly believe what I have to tell you.

Mat. Well, well, but let me hear what it is, and I'll say——

Emily. You remember the young gentleman, who so very gallantly undertook to protect me the evening I was insulted at the opera?

Mat. Remember him! How should I forget him, when you talk of nothing else?

Emily. Well, sir, he is here.

Mat. Eh? what? here? he here?

Emily. He's here! The very person who has so powerful a claim on my gratitude, is no other than Colonel Rakely.

Mat. Is it possible! and I in a manner turned him out of doors. Stop him—Shuffle—Thomas—Robert—William—stop him, where are you all?

Emily. He is still here, sir—by accident I observed him as he was leaving the house: curiosity to behold the redoubted hero led me one step forward—his eye caught mine, we recognised each other at the first glance, and for a few seconds we remained like statues fixed and mute with astonishment.

Mat. That wasn't the only emotion I warrant.

Emily. But he comes, here he is, sir, here he is.

Enter CAPTAIN BELMONT, L. H.

Bel. (*Aside.*) She here! Then come what may of it, I'll remain ; sir, I beg pardon, but on reconsidering the affair, since 'tis your humour to see me in no other than Colonel Rakely, I shall no longer object to your bestowing on me that title.

Mat. That's well, that's well! why the deuce when one has a name to be proud of, why usurp another's ?

Bel. That's exactly the reason why——

Mat. Come, come, your hand, we'll say no more about it, and to prove that I am hearty in the reconciliation, I beg pardon for the little liberties I took with your reputation. Let me present my neice to you—Lady Emily, come, come, you are old acquaintances, the introduction is hardly necessary—ha, ha, ha ! I know all about it—mmm !

Bel. Oh, madam ! could I express my delight at this unexpected meeting.

Emily. (*Curtseying.*) Sir !

Mat. Pooh! nonsense! come, none of this cold curtseying, but leave it to me. (*To Lady Emily.*) I'll arrange the affair directly.

Emily. Another match ! take care, sir, for this time perhaps——

Mat. Now, let me alone, my dear—you are fortunate Colonel in arriving to-day, for a day or two later, and Lady Emily might have appeared before you bound in the rosy fetters of wedlock.

Emily. I entreat, sir——

Mat. Why there's no harm in saying I have given a sort of promise to young Belmont.

Bel. Belmont !

Mat. Ay! an officer, a captain in your regiment. But there's nothing concluded, for he did but arrive this morning.

Bel. Arrived this morning! and before me! ha, ha !

Mat. Merely an hour or so—the truth is my dear Colonel, I had formed a little project—(*looking at him and Lady Emily.*)—but the moment you appeared——

Emily. Let me forewarn you, sir, that you must not take for granted whatever my uncle may say on this subject—as for Mr. Belmont—(*To Matchem.*) —who has neither person, fortune, nor accomplishments to recommend him, be assured he will never be my husband.

Bel. (*Aside.*) Pleasant indeed! I must discover by who I am so flatteringly represented.

Enter COLONEL from c.

Rake. So, Shuffle says that he is gone—so I may appear.

Bel. (*Aside.*) So, so, my gallant Colonel! I guess how it is—he has enjoyed a laugh at my expense, and 'tis now my turn to amuse myself a little at his.

Mat. (*Going cautiously to Rakely.*) Now be calm, be cool, be temperate, my dear Belmont—let's have no explosion here—he has confessed himself to be Colonel Rakeley, and so there's no more to be said.

Rake. (*Astonished.*) Confessed himself to be Colonel Rakely ! Oh, as he has confessed himself

to be Colonel Rakely, as you say, there is no more to be said.

Mat. That's well. (*Going to Belmont.*) There, thanks to my interference, the affair is arranged pleasantly ; he is content to overlook it.

Rake. I am happy, Colonel, ha, ha, ha ! to meet you here, Colonel ! Ha, ha, ha !

Bel. (*With an air of command.*) I sir, am more surprised than pleased at the meeting, Captain.

Rake. That air of command, ha, ha, ha ! You assume towards me, more than your usual severity, Colonel.

Bel. Have I not reason, Captain ? What do you here, sir ? I ordered you this morning on a regimental mission that required secresy and dispatch —I expect an immediate account of its result.

Rake. (*R., Aside.*) Here I am fairly caught.

Bel. Am I heard, sir ? your Colonel waits your reply.

Mat. (c.) Answer him ! Answer him !

Emily. (R. c.) Consider, sir, he is your superior officer.

Bel. (*Crossing to Lady Emily.*) I trust Lady Emily will pardon me if I am compelled to exercise my authority in her presence and under the roof of her uncle—but strict discipline and subordination must be preserved—Captain Belmont, you will instantly return to your quarters, and there wait my arrival ; your conduct shall be considered at a proper time and place.

Rake. (*Aside.*) How the devil am I to disobey—I must take the liberty—Colonel, to remonstrate against——

Bel. No parley, sir—either I am your Colonel, or I am not—answer me, sir—am I your Colonel ?

Rake. It is as certain you are my Colonel, as that I am your Captain.

Mat. For heaven's sake retire, consider discipline —subordination—court-martial—pop !

Emily. I wish you a pleasant journey, sir.

Rake. (*Aside.*) A delightful termination to my stratagem (*Crosses to L.*)

Mat. I'll order your horse to be saddled immediately—Shuffle—Shuffle I say.

Enter Shuffle, R. H.

Let Captain Belmont's horse be saddled.

Shuf. What ! he's going ? so everything's explained ?

Mat. All is explained. The Captain goes, Colonel Rakely stays.

Shuf. (*Crosses to L. H., whispers to Colonel Rakely.*) Victory, victory ! I hope I have fairly earned my twenty pounds. Captain Belmont, I'll see that your horse be ready in an instant, sir.

Mat. Eh ? what do you mean ?

Shuf. Didn't you say that all is explained and that Captain Belmont goes ?

Mat. To be sure, but that's not he, there. (*Pointing to Belmont, R.*) There's the Captain. (*To Rakely, L.*)

Shuf. How ! Then do you not yet know—Oh, blockhead that I am. (*Retires up.*)

Mat. Eh ! Why, gentlemen, will you do me the favour to explain which of you is not the other ?

Rake. For once in my life I'll be guilty of a reasonable action—Belmont, I restore you a name which if it belonged to me I should be proud of, and trust that you as well as Mr. M. will pardon me the freedom I have taken with it—as to Lady Emily, I am at a loss——

Mat. (c.) So much the better, it cuts short your speech.

Emily. (R. c.) So then *you are*——

Bel. The unhappy Belmont, who has neither person, fortune, nor accomplishments to recommend him.

Mat. And that you should be the masquerader all this while.

Rake. Confess that I am not altogether to blame; your letter to Belmont, which treated me rather hardly, excited me to a little revenge, but who could have inspired you with so ill an opinion of me ?

Mat. Your old servant, Shuffle.

Rake. So, rascal !

Shuf. Pray say no more, sir, and I'll marry the little wife you promised me, sir.

Mat. Say you so ? then I'll forgive your roguery.

Rake. And I'll give the bride away, and be father to your first boy.

Shuf. What ?

Rake. Pooh ! Godfather I mean.

Mat. That's right, Colonel, you'll pass a few days with us ; as for Belmont, he'll make rather a longer visit. I got his father married, and I hope to live to see his children married. Come, niece, never look shy about it, the young fellow has claims to your gratitude—to my friendship, and come what may of the other Match Makings, *this* I hope will succeed.

Disposition of the Characters at the Fall of the Curtain.

BEL.   EMILY.   MATCH.   SHUFFLE.   RAKELY.
R.   L.

THE DUMB BELLE.

AN ORIGINAL COMEDIETTA, IN ONE ACT.

BY WILLIAM BAYLE BERNARD.

First produced at the Royal Olympic Theatre, October 12th, 1831.

Dramatis Personæ.

[See page 6.

VIVIAN	... ...	Mr. James Vining.
MANVERS ...	... .	Mr. William Vining.
O'SMIRK ...	... ...	Mr. Brougham.
ELIZA ARDENTON	...	Madame Vestris.
MARY.	... ...	Miss Pincott.

TIME OF REPRESENTATION.—Forty-five minutes.

COSTUME.

MODERN.

STAGE DIRECTIONS.

EXITS AND ENTRANCES.—R. means *Right;* L. *Left;* D. F. *Door in Flat;* R. D. *Right Door;* L. D. *Left Door;* S. E. *Second Entrance;* U. E. *Upper Entrance;* M. D. *Middle Door;* L. U. E. *Left Upper Entrance;* R. U. E. *Right Upper Entrance;* L. S. E. *Left Second Entrance;* P. S. *Prompt Side;* O. P. *Opposite Prompt.*

RELATIVE POSITIONS.—R. means *Right;* L. *Left;* C. *Centre;* R. C. *Right of Centre;* L. C. *Left of Centre.*

    R.   R.C.   C.   L.C.   L.

*** *The Reader is supposed to be on the Stage, facing the Audience.*

THE DUMB BELLE.

SCENE.—*Parlour of a Villa, elegantly furnished. French windows at back, open on lawn and garden; a bow window,* L. H. 3 E., *contains table and chairs; doors,* R. H. *and* L., *to other apartments; table, sofa, piano, &c.*

MANVERS *discovered at table,* L. H., *looking at his watch.*

Man. No—it's past three, and no signs of him yet. What a task I've undertaken, to bring together a couple whose only resemblance is their youth and absurdity; who agree but in one thing—their constant caprice. Then, on what's my reliance? Only one hope, I own. It's a principle, I believe, that extremes produce mediums, and so, if antagonized, their opposite qualities may cause a reaction, and mutual excess lead to mutual reform. But still he delays; now that's very provoking—and here comes Eliza to make the most of the fact.

ELIZA comes from the garden.

Eliza. Well, uncle, well, who's prejudiced now?

Man. Well, certainly, Lizzy, I——

Eliza. Who now is unjust to an old and dear friend, that couldn't eat, drink, or sleep, in his ardour to see me?

Man. I own it's very strange, but——

Eliza. Who lives on my image, and, in his hurry to get here—like a horse at full speed—I suppose has run by the house?

Man. But, as I've twice said already, there must be a cause.

Eliza. Oh, of course there's a cause, which I could have told you at first—the man isn't come, because he never intended it.

Man. A solution that certainly doesn't flatter yourself, and, I think, is hard upon him, seeing he was the son of a neighbour, who only left you when his regiment was ordered abroad.

Eliza. When he packed up his memory as well as his knapsack—a man who returns, only to run off to Paris.

Man. From whence, as you're aware, he sends me a long letter——

Eliza. Which, I am also aware, you've made a point to conceal.

Man. Why, yes, my love, yes—because it's chiefly on business; but still you shall hear it—or, that is, a part of it. I can easily omit what you've no right to know, and—— (*Feeling his pockets.*) Eh? Why, it's gone!

Eliza. Well, never mind—you can remember the best of it—all that's about me.

Man. And all raptures, of course: he dwells on your memory, and the support that your image ever gave to his duties—and so I'll just ask whether such a man is not—— (*Still searching.*)

Eliza. A wretch, sir!

Man. A what, Lizzy?

Eliza. A savage—only fit for the woods he was sent to. Here is your letter, which I this morning picked up.

Man. (*Aside.*) The deuce you did!

Eliza. And, as it's so wonderfully flattering, perhaps you'll allow me to read it—not omitting those parts which I have no right to know.

Man. (*Aside.*) Now, was ever so cruel, so vile a mischance?

Eliza. (*Reads.*) "My dear Mr. Manvers, many thanks for your kindness. I am anxious, believe me to see my old home again, and also my little playmate; now changed to ;a woman, and with a mind as developed and fair as her person. I am sorry, however, to hear of one small distinction. Is it true, my dear sir, that she *talks* so incessantly? A neighbour of yours says so—says her tongue's grown proverbial—says, as you live near a station, she's called the 'Belle of the Railway!'" (There, sir—that's flattery.) I really hope he exaggerates—(generous being) for I must confess, this is a point on which I'm grown rather sensitive—I can't tell you what I've suffered from talkative woman. (How very deplorable.) Our quartermaster's wife had a tongue like a roll call—and so had the major's, and the doctor's to boot. (Poor soul!) And, now I'm in Paris, my fate's just as bad—they actually talk me to death, sir! (There—there's a martyr!) So, you really mustn't wonder if I've been forced into wishing that some of her sex were born dumb, (dumb! do you hear? dumb!) as a refuge for the victims of their clamorous sisters. A young and sensible dumb woman I could fancy invaluable, and I shouldn't at all scruple to run half over Europe to——" but there—there's your raptures, sir—I've had enough of 'em.

(*Throwing down the letter; he picks it up.*)

Man. Well, certainly, Eliza, I can't but acknowledge——

Eliza. You're laughing—actually laughing at this monster's impertinence!

Man. No, no—on the contrary, I'm convinced that he thinks you——

Eliza. The "Belle of the Railway," — much obliged to him, certainly!

Man. But you must see through this nonsense, that it's a mere moment's folly; and if it doesn't affect his real feelings towards you——

Eliza. You'll, of course, not object to put that fact to the proof: since he comes with such notions, I'm resolved he shall test them; since he would run half over Europe to discover a dumb woman, he shall be satisfied *here.*

Man. Here!

Eliza. Here—*I* will oblige him.

Man. Now, now, Eliza—

Eliza. Nay, nay—you've no right to refuse, after the trick of that letter; and you must own he deserves one for its precious contents—so, you must say, "Yes" at once, when I will tell you my scheme, and—

(*O'Smirk is heard outside in the garden.*)

O'Smirk. Oh, very well, very well—only show me the door, and—

Man. Eh—an arrival?

(*He appears at back with carpet-bag, coats, &c.*)

O'Smirk. The top of the morning to every one present. Is it Mr. Manvers I've the honour to spake to?

Man. Yes—Mr. Manvers.

O'Smirk. Then, I hope before long, sir, we shall be better acquainted.

Man. But pray, may I ask——

O'Smirk. Who I am! Oh, you may, sir—that's natural enough. Well, sir, I'm a man that I'll engage you'll like better, the better you know me.

Man. Perhaps so—but, in the meantime, as I suppose you're a master——

O'Smirk. A master! Of course, sir, and a nate lad he is—a very sensible—well-behaved boy, I assure you—tho' you'll say it's no wonder, seeing I've been with him this five years, and—

Man. And pray what's detained him?

O'Smirk. As dirty a reason as you'd guess in a month, sir—as pretty a ditch as ever gaped for a breakfast.

Man. A ditch!

O'Smirk. Yes, a ditch, sir—or, that's to say, half of it, for we shared it betwixt us, as we had done the post-chaise. By way of knowing the country—we rowled into a hole, and——

Man. And so all's explained. Well, there's his room, where you can put down his things, and, of course, as he's coming——

Eliza. (*Aside.*) We'll go and prepare, uncle.

Man. Nay, nay—not a step till I know your design.

Eliza. And you shall, sir, you shall. You're fond of the arts, and you shall judge of my design when you see the execution.

[*They go off by* L. H. *door.*

O'Smirk. And that's the darling, is it, that he's coming to see here, that has got such a clapper. Well, and more power to it! Is it for a soldier to quarrel with the music it makes,—when let it roll as it likes, it's a hint for saluting.

(*Vivian is heard outside at back.*)

Viv. Hallo! Gate, gate!

O'Smirk. Eh—there's my master: so I must put down his traps, and then find out the kitchen. It's yonder, I smell it. I know no better subaltern than an Irishman's nose, when the service he's on is to recruit the main body.

[*He goes into room,* R. H.

Viv. No one coming—very well. I used to jump over it—try again !

He enters at back with a bound, and advances.

MANVERS *enters from* L. H. *door.*

Cleared it, by Jove! Only six paces, and—ah, my old friend !

Man. Welcome, Henry, welcome—a dozen welcomes to Harewood !

Viv. And one from your hand is worth a dozen elsewhere. Well, and how have you been, sir, during our long separation? You see I'm not altered—remember all my old tricks—my cool way of entering your friendly domain. Nor do I see a change here—every .tree, every flower-pot stands where I left it, and I could almost swear, too, that —there are the identical sunflowers that waved their adieux to me.

Man. You've not forgot your romance, Henry?

Viv. Hardly, sir, hardly, if that means my sympathy with nature and man. Well—and where's Eliza?

Man. She'll be here presently.

Viv. To prove to me, of course, how poor a painter is fame.

Man. I think so, indeed.

Viv. She's had throngs of admirers?

Man. They've been like motes in the sunbeam.

Viv. Or a flight of Indian arrows that darken the day.

Man. for which reason, I suppose, you'll infer she's not caught one.

Viv. That or another. I did hear another cause; but we can't expect perfection; the best must have some defects: and so young and so clever, and so exceedingly charming, one can hardly complain if she has one little fault; though, oddly enough, it's just that I object to, as my letter explained—didn't offend you, I hope?

Man. Oh, not at all.

Viv. I stated, as you perceived, sir, my peculiar experience—my singular sufferings from a certain propensity; but that was among strangers: with an old friend, of course. I should make due allowance: with an old friend I trust I should endure an affliction which——

Man. Which you'll never encounter.

Viv. What, sir?

Man. It's time to make known to you a very sad piece of news—to tell you she has met with a very serious calamity.

Viv. A calamity !

Man. Yes—that on the lakes, some months since, she was upset in a boat—when the cold and the terror striking through her together, fastened, at length, upon her throat, and deprived her of speech.

Viv. What do you say?

Man. Deprived her of speech—at this moment she is tongue-tied.

Viv. What, Eliza?

Man. Eliza—you can't get a word from her.

Viv. Ha! ha! ha! Why my dear Mr. Manvers, I'm perfectly enraptured !

Man. Enraptured !

Viv. That is, at her escape, sir—her escape, sir, of course.

Man. She's had all the best advice, as you'll easily suppose; but as some months have elapsed, and the defect still continues——

Viv. Yes, sir—continues.

Man. I now begin to doubt that she'll ever recover.

Viv. You're certain of that—don't think she'll recover.

Man. I doubt it, indeed.

Viv. Ha! ha! poor thing—dear soul—how very affecting—how delighted I am to—to offer my sympathy! (*Aside.*) A dumb girl—a dumb girl—

a young and sensible dumb girl—I've found her at last.

Man. So, I hope you'll excuse my reserve on this point, as I was really afraid it might——

Viv. Might what, sir? It charms me—it draws me towards her—makes me eager to congratulate—I mean to condole with her; so go to her, I beg, sir—let her know that I'm here, and panting to peak to her.

Man. Yes, yes; but you've only heard *half* her calamity : the cold has seized on her hearing—she's deaf, as well as dumb.

Viv. Well, and what of that, sir?

Man. Why, as her ears have a sinecure as well as her lips——

Viv. Her eyes are still left me—her eyes, sir, her eyes : and would you compare their intelligence with that of the tongue—light itself—electricity with poor crawling sound——

Man. Well, that I know, but——

Viv. Her eyes, sir, that pause not to frame signs for the soul, but reveal it at once.

Man. And you actually pretend you'd be willing to marry——

Viv. To marry—to worship her—devote my whole life to her—sing to her—play to her—dance, if she wished it—till thus grown united in thought and in feeling, one pulse and one mainspring should link heart to heart.

Man. And are you then serious?

Viv. Serious! I'm frantic, sir!

Man. But, my dear boy, consider——

Viv. My fever! Go, go, sir.

Man. A deaf and dumb woman——

Viv. Extacy—extacy!

Man. Who never can say to you——

Viv. Raptures! Oh, go, sir.

(*Pushes him out through* L. H. *door, and walks about.* O'Smirk *comes from* R. H. *door.*)

But can this be truth—Eliza this treasure—the girl I've avoided the very one I would find? She the being—the angel who would convey the assurance that——

O'Smirk. Your clane shirt is ready, sir.

Viv. Shirts! Don't talk of shirts to a man who's scarce conscious he's wearing a body. Phelim, get ready for a run up to town. I shall be married in a month.

O'Smirk. Married, sir!

Viv. Married—and to whom—guess to whom—my own loved Eliza. She is the being I have sought for so long—an intellectual dumb woman!

O'Smirk. A dumb woman!

Viv. Yes, that *rara avis in terra.*

O'Smirk. Why, then, by my soul, she'd be a terror to any one.

Viv. So you shall run up, to-morrow, order a travelling carriage, and——

O'Smirk. Oh, be aisy, be aisy, sir.

Viv. I say I'm resolved, sir.

O'Smirk. Ye are—mighty fine; but just tell me this. When the clargyman bids her say that she'll love and obey you, how's she to do it?

Viv. I suppose she could nod, sir?

O'Smirk. Nod is it—nod; and ye'd have a wife nodding instead of opening her lips? Mightn't ye as well marry a head in a tay shop? Suppose, sir, she were to bring you a little brood of Chinese mandarins, sir, stuck in every hole and corner, and doing nothing all day but nodding their heads at ye.

Viv. Silence, you raven, and bring me my boots! Every moment I delay is a treason to Eliza. Oh, with that name how childhood comes back with all its early freshness, and the future brightens with a richer smile. Get out, you villain.

[*Kicks him into* R. H. *room, and follows.*

(MARY *looks in from garden, then enters, followed by* ELIZA, *with a reticule, which she puts on table in bow window.*)

Mary. All's safe ; he's in his room, miss.

Eliza. Then now I may enter, with my little auxiliaries.

(*She takes an ear trumpet and note book from her bag, and places them on table.*)

Well, Mary, you've seen him, and how does he look? Grown a great fright, of course? Round shouldered—short necked—hair, a fine furze bush—and skin a deep snuff colour.

Mary. Oh, no, ma'am, he hasn't ; his skin is quite clean—got a natural blush in it.

Eliza. Well, I'm glad to hear that, for it's certainly wanted.

Mary. And so you really intend, miss, to be dumb all to-day?

Eliza. Yes, all to-day.

Mary. But—but are you sure, miss, you can?

Eliza. Can, indeed! Can!

Mary. Why, you know, you never tried ; so to make sure, wouldn't it be as well just to practice a little?

Eliza. So you believe I love chattering as much as yourself ; to prove to you the contrary, I'll be dumb from this moment ; mind, I don't speak another word after I've told you to go. Mary, go. (*She turns away to table. Mary is going off.*) Mary!

Mary. Yes, miss.

Eliza. Bless me, I forgot. It's really not so easy a thing as I thought. Well, and now for the trial. If he proves the sort of man that his letter implies, why restraint will be easy, and silence agreeable ; but if, on the contrary, I should find all this folly to be merely affected, why then I'm afraid that the first time he murmurs "Poor afflicted Eliza!" I shall surprise him by saying—"Oh, my dear Henry, how glad I am to see you."

MANVERS *comes from* L. H. *door.*

Man. Now, Eliza, are you ready?

Eliza. Yes, uncle, quite ; only Mary, you know, you've to take charge of his servant ; take him to the kitchen, or do what you like, only keep him away.

Mary. He shall have an obstacle, miss, that he'll never get over—a shoulder of mutton.

(*Eliza seating herself at table in bow window.* Manvers *taps at* R. H. *door.*)

Man. Now, Harry, may I enter?

Viv. Of course, sir, or I'll come to you ; and now——

(*He comes out, followed by* O'Smirk, *to whom Mary beckons ; they go off at back.*)

Lead me to the dear one—to our own loved Eliza ! Do I see her—it must be—yet how changed—how improved !—Fame—fame has slandered her. She's an angel !

(*He advances—she turns and extends her hand to him, which he kisses ; leading her forward.*)

Dear Eliza, you know not the joy that this meeting affords me—joy tempered with sympathy—with the profoundest regret. Though parted so long, and by the space of wide oceans, be assured they'd no power to bury the past! your face was ever present to me, your eyes, and your thoughts, like the same moon and stars, which——

(Vivian pausing, Eliza goes to table, takes up the ear trumpet, and returning to his side, puts it to her ear, and nods.)

Man. You must say that again.

Viv. Through a trumpet?

Man. Didn't I tell you that the cold had deprived her of hearing?

Viv. Oh, I forgot. My dearest Eliza——

Man. A little louder.

Viv. My dearest Eliza——

Man. Too low.

Viv. Would you have me alarm the neighbourhood?

Man. Oh, they've got used to it.

Viv. *(Shouting.)* My angelic Eliza——

(Eliza nods her head and smiles.)

Man. Ah, now she hears you.

Viv. Well, I should think so.

Man. Proceed.

Viv. After our long separation——

Man. You're sinking again.

Viv. *(Bawling.)* After our long separation, you can't imagine the joy I now feel to address you.

Man. What do you say?

Viv. Well, sir?

Man. Consider her affliction; you mean to say the pain you now feel to address her.

Viv. Well, there's no lie in that.

Man. Go on.

Viv. I can't.

Man. Is your heart so very full?

Viv. No! My lungs are so empty.

(Eliza goes to the table, sits and writes.)

Man. She will write you a reply.

Viv. Write! Well, of course; that never struck me—and of all things in the world, an epistolary correspondence is what I like most—*(Eliza comes forward and gives him tablets—reads.)* "I am truly delighted to see my old friend, and regret I cannot say so." Oh, never heed that, never mind your tongue, dear Eliza, I read it in your eyes——

Man. You know that can't be heard.

Viv. *(Shouting.)* Never mind your tongue, dear Eliza. Oh d——n it, this is too ridiculous!

Man. Well, well, you now know how to communicate, so as I've a letter to write, I'll leave you together.

(He goes off at the back; she stands twirling the trumpet.)

Vir. What a horrible nuisance! We must do without that, or I must go a sea voyage, and take a lesson in hailing—learn to bawl as if I was telling her to pull down her jib. We surely could light upon some other means to—our fingers! Of course, we must learn to talk with them—that's the plan. The first week of our marriage we'll pass in a dumb school; but what to do now—now. Why, I'll write—I'll write, and she'll answer. Yes, yes, I—*(going to table at back; he takes up drawings.)* Views of the lake! And how exquisite—all of them. Are these yours, Eliza, yours? *(He makes signs to her; she nods in return.)* Come, we're getting on; that's the way to talk to her! Natural pantomime. Yes, treasured scenes, sacred ever to memory, here you live again as you first met my senses. Do you remember this, Lizzy, our old summer ramble, when, with hearts like the breeze, we ran off together, and—*(Eliza taps his shoulder, and puts up the trumpet.)* What an ass to forget; but we may as well sit; after such exertion one's rather exhausted. *(He brings chairs, and they seat themselves.)* I've a thousand things to say to you, and as I see you've your tablets. *(She again puts up her trumpet.)* No, no—not that; we must converse without that: feelings like ours protest against mechanism—it destroys all emotion, not to say health. No, no—no art: if we must have a resource, let me rather go to nature—let me adopt the old primitive mode of the sand-bag—ahoy! *(Exemplifying—he takes the trumpet from her, which she parts with unwillingly.)* Do you remember, Eliza—oh, I'm too low! *(Bawling.)* You remember Colonel Johnson—heard he was married—yes, married in Paris—a nice little woman—couple of excellent souls. *(She nods and writes, then hands him the tablets—reads.)* "Yes, soles are very excellent, but they're not in the market." In the market, my darling! I didn't mean fish—ahem! You remember the Wilsons—piano again! *(Bawling.)* You remember the Wilsons—heard of their failure—the general distress? *(She nods and writes rapidly.)* Ah! understands me this time; thought we should do without that infernal conductor—a conductor, by-the-bye, that doesn't lead to a bus. *(She hands him the tablet, wiping her eyes.)* Dear soul, how it affects her! She loved the Wilsons, I know. *(Reads.)* "Yes, I do well remember the general distress: poor little Pompey was everyone's favourite." D——n little Pompey! Have I been threatening my blood-vessels on account of a poodle? *(A dinner bell rings outside, violently. Vivian claps his hands to his ears; Eliza takes no notice.)* Hallo! What's the matter? House on fire! Stop! Eliza! Eliza, don't you hear some one ringing? *(He makes signs of a bell ringing violently, which she doesn't understand.)* Gracious powers! Not hear that: then we must have the conductor. Eliza, my darling, put up your trumpet. *(He gives it to her; she listens, then nods and writes.)* And now I shall hear what all that noise was about. *(She gives him the tablets, then rises, and goes out through L. H. door—reads.)* "I've a young friend in the next room who always rings the alarm bell when she wishes to see me—pray excuse me a moment." Rings the alarm bell! A comfortable house this, with an alarm bell and a speaking trumpet going all day. If this is their quiet, what do they call a disturbance? Talk of my old quarters; why when did even Billingsgate make such a clangor? Besides, there the noise is natural —at least it is human, and—*(Eliza sings in the next room.)* Why, how charming! How that voice floated towards me, as some spirit that glides here to calm this confusion. And that is her friend! Ah, if 'twere herself! If she breathed these sounds—because I do not object to singing, though I do to a chatter. Music and uproar are very distinct things; and yet, of course, if a woman's dumb, she isn't able to sing. Now, that's a great bore! Why can't a woman sing, and not be able to talk?

MANVERS *returns from the back.*

Man. You'll excuse my delay, but—oh, where's Eliza.

Vir. Gone to her friend in the next room; a young lady that sings.

Man. Sings!

Viv. And divinely. I think I never listened to a voice so entrancing—such feeling—such sweetness.

Man. But what's this to you? I thought your great object was to discover a dumb woman?

Viv. Dumb, did I say? Dumb—or comparatively dumb.

Man. Dumb said your letter.

Viv. I really think you mistake! I think I said comparatively—that the passage ran thus—"I wish 'twere possible for women to be comparatively dumb, that they might sing, but not speak."

Man. Sing!

Viv. Oh, yes, sing. I said sing, because music's my passion—comparatively dumb—that they might sing but not speak; you see these are nice distinctions.

Man. Very, indeed.

Viv. And of course I shall have the pleasure of meeting this lady!

Man. Meeting her! Hardly! She's going away to avoid you.

Viv. To avoid me!

Man. Of course, we especially begged it.

Viv. And why, pray?

Man. Because the girl chatters; and tho' her voice is a soft one, yet remembering your sufferings——

Viv. But not from soft voices! Loud talking is my horror; that's your mistake, sir; a soft and low voice I should never object to—indeed, I should prefer it to absolute silence.

Man. (*Aside.*) So, so; it's begun.

Viv. A soft and low voice would give a charming variety, and you've sent her away because—why, how rude she must think me! I ought to go after her, and make an apology.

(*Going off*, L. II.—*Manvers seizes him.*)

Man. No, no—there's no occasion.

Viv. But, my dear sir, there is—in your zeal for my comfort, you've injured my character—you've offered an insult which I'm bound to retract—bound as a gentleman to regret—and atone for, and—— (MARY *is seen crossing the garden at back, in an elegant cloak and bonnet.*) Eh—why, who's that?

Man. That! Why, that's her, on her way to her carriage.

Viv. And no one escorting her—why, worse, sir, and worse——

Man. (*Holding him.*) But you mustn't do it—for you know you're a stranger——

Viv. Not to civility—I really must go, sir——

Man. But I've said you'd avoid her.

Viv. Well, sir, that's your fault.

Man. And as she is reserved——

Viv. Well—and that's hers.

Man. But here comes Eliza.

Viv. But you can excuse me.

Man. But what shall I say to her?

Viv. Say, sir! Why, say that——

ELIZA *enters from* L. II. *door hastily, and puts up her trumpet.*

Confound that conductor! [*He runs off at back.*]

Eliza. Ha! ha! And now, uncle, what do you think of my scheme?

Man. It succeeds, beyond doubt;—he has run after Miss Rivers.

Eliza. Under which gentle name, my Mary will lead him a chase round the grounds, and at length bring him back to be exposed on this spot.

Man. I own he deserves it.

Eliza. Deserves it, indeed! A creature who gives up the substance for shadow, and will endure in a stranger what he denies to a friend! I thought my japan, here, would bring him to reason.

Man. And that done—what do you think of him?

Eliza. Oh, the man's well enough—but I could scarcely enjoy a talk which he had all to himself.

Man. Why, no, Lizzy, no.

Eliza. Or be in the happiest of moods whilst enduring such agony.

Man. Agony!

Eliza. Yes—to keep my tongue quiet; I had to bite it till it bled.

Man. What singular courage? Talk of the boy and the wolf——

Eliza. So you see I'm entitled to some compensation—and may honestly tax you for further assistance—to follow him to the grounds, and delay his pursuit till Mary's enabled to return to the house.

Man. When, of course, he will enter it——

Eliza. Like a criminal into court, to be duly convicted. Now you see what's my aim, to assert the rights of our sex; let me but force him to own them, to confess that our speech is a sacred possession——

Man. And then, I suppose——

Eliza. I may reward him with mine for the rest of his days. [*He goes off at the back.*] Yes, Mr. Harry, I think you'll meet with a proper exposure. Here Mary shall sit, duly veil'd, on her return, and here, you'll approach to enjoy a *tête-à-tête.* She'll remain silent—you'll beg her to speak—and then when I looking in—(*O'Smirk looks in from the garden*)—you implore her to utter one merciful word—I shall promptly repay you with a flood from myself.

O'Smirk. Pillaloo!

Eliza. (*Turning.*) Oh, la!

O'Smirk. And is it you are the dumb lady, ma'am, if you plase.

Eliza. (*Aside.*) Was ever anything so provoking?

O'Smirk. Is it you that can't spake for the cowld that you caught? 'Pon my word, then, I never heard such a beautiful whisper.

Eliza. (*Aside.*) Now all's at an end; my whole scheme is overthrown.

O'Smirk. Oh, it's no use, my lady, to nod your head now, ma'am; if you're dumb, only say so, only say that you're dumb, and I'll be dumb with joy myself for the rest of the day.

Eliza. Well, it's no use disguising, but you'll surely not betray me; my secret is safe with you.

O'Smirk. Safe with me, ma'am! Is it an Irishman you spake to? By my sowl, it's as safe with me as a keg of bad cyder.

Eliza. Especially when you're aware of the end I have in view, which is to cure your master of his present unnatural taste.—I'm sure you'd never wish that our sex should be speechless.

O'Smirk. Spacheless, the darlings! Would I rob the world of its music, or man of his monitor? Ain't the women our watches? and would I have 'em stop ticking?

Eliza. Ah! What a thought! Then, perhaps, you'd do more, you'd not object to assist me?

O'Smirk. Do what, ma'am?

Eliza. To take the place of my maid, and represent a young lady?

O'Smirk. A young lady!

Eliza. Yes—an interesting girl, who's in delicate health.

O'Smirk. Oh, nothing's more aisy.

Eliza. Why, how kind of you—how charming! Then as soon as she enters——

                (MARY *runs in from the garden.*)

Mary. Oh, miss, are you there! Such a terrible chase!

Eliza. But you escaped him, I hope?

Mary. Yes, and that's all—for he ran like a greyhound twice round the shrubbery, and all through the maze, and but for my master—— (*Sees* O'Smirk.) Eh? bless me!

Eliza. Never fear, he's our friend—who will strengthen my project by taking your place; so, whilst I array him, do you, Mary, keep watch.

Mary. And Mr. O'Smirk to be a lady of fashion.

O'Smirk. And ain't he the boy for it? Isn't she a sharp shooter—and don't both of us know how to bring a man on his knees?

                (Mary *surrendering the cloak and bonnet, goes to back—Eliza arrays* O'Smirk.)

Eliza. Now your master, you see, will be here in an instant; but my uncle will follow to prevent a discovery.

O'Smirk. You're certain of that? Not that I mind a kicking, but it would be a pity, you know, to spoil such a nice cloak.

Eliza. Never fear! That will do! And really that's famous—why, you might pass for a female —on a very dark night.

O'Smirk. Oh, I might—and be run after by half the police.

Eliza. And now, here's your seat—here are drawings to engage you—to divert your attention —and——

                (*He sits at table at bow-window, she arranging the cloak and bonnet.*)

Mary. If you please, miss, he's coming.

Eliza. Very good—then we'll go; now be cautious—be cautious!

Mary. And, do, pray sit up? Whoever saw a lady sprawl about so?

O'Smirk. Oh, be aisy—be aisy, don't it show I've a taste; here's beautiful pictures, and ain't I bound to go over 'em?

                (*They go off through* L. H. *door as* VIVIAN *comes from the garden.*)

Viv. No, not on the lawn; so she must have run in; why what is this mystery—what can they have said to her to cause all this terror? She couldn't have run faster to escape a mad bull—I'll have an explanation, let it cost what it may, and—Eh? There she sits; her own charming person. Exquisite being!

O'Smirk. (*Aside.*) That's me.

Viv. What a fool must be he that would dispense with your faculty.

O'Smirk. (*Aside.*) And the fool is my master.

Viv. Fortune's my friend; and I'll not be ungrateful. I believe I've the honour of addressing Miss Rivers?

O'Smirk. Ahem!

Viv. I trust she'll pardon this abruptness, but as I fear that she's labouring under some signal delusion, some belief to my prejudice which I am bound to remove, will she allow me to state that some half hour since I listened to her singing—to a voice so enchanting that I fairly forgot everything but the desire to thank her.

O'Smirk. (*Aside.*) Oh, the cracher! Ahem!
                (*He shakes his leg and head.*)

Viv. (*Aside.*) Why, she's trembling; yes trembling—what can cause this emotion? The mystery of this being increases every instant. Now, why can't she speak? What's the use of a tongue if a woman won't use it? What a treason to nature— to silence, a faculty which——

MANVERS *enters from the garden.*

Man. And so, Harry, I've caught you.

Viv. (*Aside.*) Plague take it—now he's here.

Man. And by the side of this lady! Now what does this mean? I thought, sir, your aim was to discover a dumb woman?

Viv. Yes, but not a deaf one; I never said deaf, sir; one I could never talk to but through a yard of japan, nor breathe the fondest wish to, but in the tone of a bassoon.

Man. What's this?

Viv. That I couldn't love without letting the whole parish know it, nor praise without scaring the cats on the tiles.

Man. But permit me to say this is a change in your sentiments.

Viv. Not at all, sir, not at all—imagine a man's fate who's linked to such a being; robbed of all social and intellectual pleasure, because robbed of speech; conceive him for instance at any great crisis: say he enters her room after a certain joyful event—he finds her, dear girl, in a state of touching exhaustion—of pensive composure—of sweet and soft dishabille—everything is hushed down to the song of the kettle—the nurse treads like a fairy, and breathes like a zephyr; then, when she looks up to him for kind consolation, he must shout in her ears, "Eliza, my darling, pray how's the baby?" Oh, confound it!

Man. I see, sir, your meaning; you're in love with Miss Rivers, and merely because she can sing.

Viv. Sing! Hang her singing! Because she can talk, sir. I wouldn't marry a woman wanting an eye or a leg; and why wanting speech? Speech, the great distinction that divides us from brutes; brutes, sir, can see; man only can talk.

Man. And in the case of a woman, no matter how loudly.

Viv. Not a bit, sir, occasionally; if she always talked softly she might grow monotonous — might weary us, like the sky of the South with its brightness: a cloud, as in England, gives brightness its zest; and so a quarrel in wedlock might stir up affection.

Man. Well, this is a change, certainly; and if it's likely to last——

Viv. To last!—As a rock, sir. Nothing can shake it.

Man. Then here comes Eliza to encounter its shock.

ELIZA *comes from the garden, followed by* MARY.

Viv. And the sooner it's over, sir, the happier for all of us; though, in addition, I must tell you there are many other reasons why I never could marry her.

Man. Many others!

Viv. Yes, sir; she may have grown out of them, but, you know, when a child, she had all the tricks of a wild cat.

Man. Hollo! Softly—softly.

Viv. What's the matter? She can't hear me, you know: then that defect in her eyes hasn't worn off at all; rather increased, sir—she squints!

Man. Squints! Hush, for Heaven's sake!

Viv. But, above all, she has a defect which, with me, settles the matter. I heard, on the honour of a Guardsman who waltzed with her lately, that she has infernally thick legs.

Eliza. What do you say?

Viv. Eliza!

Eliza. You monster!

Viv. She speaks!

Eliza. And enough to make one, you horrible villifier!

Viv. Oh, ye lakes, let me run to you, and hide my confusion!

Eliza. No, no, sir; not before you've enjoyed, at least, one of your wishes—an introduction to Miss Rivers, whom you're dying to know.

(*She takes off the bonnet from O'Smirk.*)

Viv. Phelim! You scoundrel!

O'Smirk. Don't say that, sir, I beg. I'll do you justice to say you made love like an Irishman.

Viv. So I've been prettily laughed at, it seems, after all. Well, I won't deny 'twas deserved; but, as the lesson's been given, you'll allow me, at least, to endure it elsewhere. (*He is going off at back.*)

Eliza. Henry!

Viv. (*Turning.*) Eliza!

Eliza. After six years' separation, did I think you'd trust to slanders, rather than judge for yourself, or, in our first hour of meeting, would desert an old friend at the mere voice of a stranger.

Viv. I cannot defend it.

Eliza. Your letter to my uncle suggested my stratagem; but what was the result? A proof that you're incapable of any lasting attachment.

Viv. But not of compunction, or respect for your feelings; and as I cannot hope to be forgiven——

Eliza. Do you wish to be forgiven?

Viv. Can you ask it?

Eliza. Then kneel, sir. (*He does so.*) Are you sorry—very sorry for all the libels you've uttered on that privilege of the sex which ranks among the oldest of earth's institutions?

Viv. I am,

Eliza. Do you confess, with your whole heart, that it's right to be exercised; and not only that—but that it is as pleasant for man to bear, as for woman to minister?

Viv. I do.

Eliza. And will you evermore maintain this invaluable creed—against all social heretics, of all classes whatever; whether autocratic fathers, revolutionary husbands, anarchical brothers, or barbarized bachelors?

Viv. I will.

Eliza. Then rise, sir; I forgive you.

Viv. And may I really believe you are so allied to an angel that——

Eliza. (*Puts up her trumpet.*) Speak a little louder, Harry.

Viv. Oh, confound that conductor! Throw it away, I beseech you.

Eliza. I must first ask the consent of those who are around me. (*To the audience.*) My experiment in one case, it seems, is successful; will it prove so in all? May I hope, in consideration of all I've suffered to-day—I'm sure the ladies will feel for me—its faults may be forgiven? And, now the "Dumb Belle" has recovered her speech, she will never again need the aid of her little assistant.

CURTAIN.

MUSIC.

DICKS' PIANOFORTE TUTOR.

This book is full music size, and contains instructions and exercises, full of simplicity and melody, which will not weary the student in their study, thus rendering the work the best Pianoforte Guide ever issued. It contains as much matter as those tutors for which six times the amount is charged. The work is printed on toned paper of superior quality, in good and large type. Price One Shilling; post free, Twopence extra.

CZERNY'S STUDIES FOR THE PIANOFORTE.

These celebrated Studies in precision and velocity, for which the usual price has been Half-a-Guinea, is now issued at One Shilling; post free, threepence extra. Every student of the Pianoforte ought to possess this companion to the tutor to assist him at obtaining proficiency on the instrument.

DICKS' EDITION OF STANDARD OPERAS (full music size), with Italian, French, or German and English Words. Now ready:—

DONIZETTI'S "LUCIA DI LAMMERMOOR," with Portrait and Memoir of the Composer. Price 2s. 6d.
ROSSINI'S "IL BARBIERE," with Portrait and Memoir of the Composer. Price 2s. 6d.
Elegantly bound in cloth, gilt lettered, 5s. each. Others are in the Press. Delivered carriage free for Eighteenpence extra per copy to any part of the United Kingdom.

SIMS REEVES' SIX CELEBRATED TENOR SONGS, Music and Words. Price One Shilling. Pilgrim of Love. Bishop.—Death of Nelson. Braham.—Adelaide, Beethoven.—The Thorn. Shield. —The Anchor's Weighed. Braham.—Tell me, Mary, how to Woo Thee. Hodson.

ADELINA PATTI'S SIX FAVOURITE SONGS, Music and Words. Price One Shilling. There be none of Beauty's Daughters. Mendelssohn.—Hark, hark, the Lark. Schubert.—Home, Sweet Home. Bishop.—The Last Rose of Summer. T. Moore.—Where the Bee Sucks. Dr. Arne.—Tell me, my Heart. Bishop.

CHARLES SANTLEY'S SIX POPULAR BARITONE SONGS. Music and Words. Price One Shilling. The Lads of the Village. Dibdin.—The Wanderer. Schubert.—In Childhood My Toys. Lortzing. —Tom Bowling. Dibdin.—Rock'd in the Cradle of the Deep. Knight.—Mad Tom. Purcell.
₊ Any of the above Songs can also be had separately, price Threepence each.

MUSICAL TREASURES.— Full Music size, price Fourpence. Now Publishing Weekly. A Complete Repertory of the best English and Foreign Music, ancient and modern, vocal and instrumental, solo and concerted, with critical and biographical annotations, for the pianoforte.

1 My Normandy (Ballad)
2 Auld Robin Gray (Scotch Ballad)
3 La Sympathie Valse
4 The Pilgrim of Love (Romance)
5 Di Pescatore (Song)
6 To Far-off Mountain (Duet)
7 The Anchor's Weigh'd (Ballad)
8 A Woman's Heart (Ballad)
9 Oh, Mountain Home! (Duet)
10 Above, how Brightly Beams the Morning
11 The Marriage of the Roses (Valse)
12 Norma (Duet)
13 Lo! Heavenly Beauty (Cavatina)
14 In Childhood my Toys (Song)
15 While Beauty Clothes the Fertile Vale
16 The Harp that once through Tara's Halls
17 The Manly Heart (Duet)
18 Beethoven's "Andante and Variations"
19 In that Long-lost Home we Love (Song)
20 Where the Bee Sucks (Song)
21 Ah, Fair Dream ("Marta")
22 La Petit Fleur
23 Angels ever Bright and Fair
24 Naught e'er should Sever (Duet)
25 'Tis but a little Faded Flow'r (Ballad)
26 My Mother bids me Bind my Hair (Canzonet)
27 Coming thro' the Rye (Song)
28 Beautiful Isle of the Sea (Ballad)
29 Tell me, my Heart (Song)
30 I know a Bank (Duet)
31 The Minstrel Boy (Irish Melody)
32 Hommage au Genie
33 See what Pretty Brooms I've Bought
34 Tom Bowling (Song)
35 Tell me, Mary, how to Woo Thee (Ballad)
36 When the Swallows Homeward Fly (Song)
37 Rock'd in the Cradle of the Deep (Song)
38 Beethoven's Waltzes First Series
39 As it Fell upon a Day (Duet)
40 A Life on the Ocean Wave (Song)
41 Why are you Wandering here I pray? (Ballad)
42 A Maiden's Prayer.
43 Valse Brillante
44 Home, Sweet Home! (Song)
45 Oft in the Stilly Night (Song)
46 All's Well (Duet)
47 The "Crown Diamonds" Fantasia
48 Hear me, dear One (Serenade)
49 Youth and Love at the Helm (Barcarolle)
50 Adelaide Beethoven (Song)
51 The Death of Nelson (Song)
52 Hark, hark, the Lark
53 The Last Rose of Summer (Irish Melody)
54 The Thorn (Song)
55 The Lads of the Village (Song)
56 There be none of Beauty's Daughters (Song)
57 The Wanderer (Song)
58 I have Plucked the Fairest Flower
59 Bid Me Discourse (Song)
60 Fisher Maiden (Song)
61 Fair Agnes (Barcarolle)
62 How Calm and Bright (Song)
63 Woman's Inconstancy (Song)
64 Echo Duet
65 The Meeting of the Waters (Irish Melody)
66 Lo, Here the Gentle Lark
67 Beethoven's Waltzes (Second Series)
68 Child of Earth with the Golden Hair (Song)
69 Should he Upbraid (Song)

London: JOHN DICKS, 313, Strand; and all Booksellers.

www.ingramcontent.com/pod-product-compliance
Lightning Source LLC
Chambersburg PA
CBHW021459090426
42739CB00009B/1794